Published by Mz. Kim Productions
4263 Tierra Rejada Rd #151
Moorpark, CA 93021
www.mzkimproductions.com
ISBN: 978-1-962106-01-6

Printed in United States of America
First Printing: August 2023
Date of Copyright: July 5, 2023

Cover design by Veronika Wilson (Techflames LLC)
Illustrations by Veronika Wilson (Techflames LLC)

For permissions, please contact: Mz. Kim Productions
4263 Tierra Rejada Rd #151
Moorpark, CA 93021
www.mzkimproductions.com
mzkimproductions@gmail.com

I0457646

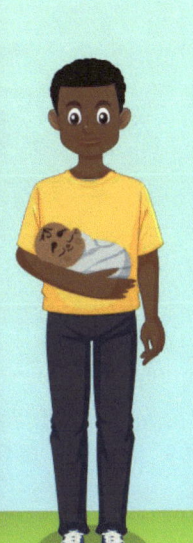

Once upon a time, in a town filled with love and laughter, there lived a young boy named Gio and his loving mother, Ebony.

Gio loved spending time with his mother, learning about life's wonders. One day, Ebony shared a special book called the Bible with Gio.

The Bible was filled with words of wisdom and love, just like a treasure chest of guidance for Gio.

Every night, Gio would sit by his window, gazing at the stars, and read the Bible passages his mother had shared with him.

As Gio read, he felt his mother's love surrounding him, like a guardian angel watching over him.

One day, Gio faced a challenge—a deep, rushing river. But he remembered his mother's words and found courage in the Bible.

With his mother's love guiding him, Gio crossed the river, knowing he was never alone.

Years passed, and Gio became a father himself. He shared the Bible's teachings with his child, passing down the legacy of love and faith.

Together, they discovered the timeless wisdom of the Bible, finding comfort and hope in its words.

The story of Gio and his guardian angel became a cherished tale in their town, reminding everyone of the enduring power of love.

And so, they lived their lives, knowing that love, like the bond between Gio and his mother, is a gift that never fades away.

And in their hearts, they carried the love of Gio's guardian angel, guiding them through life's joys and sorrows.

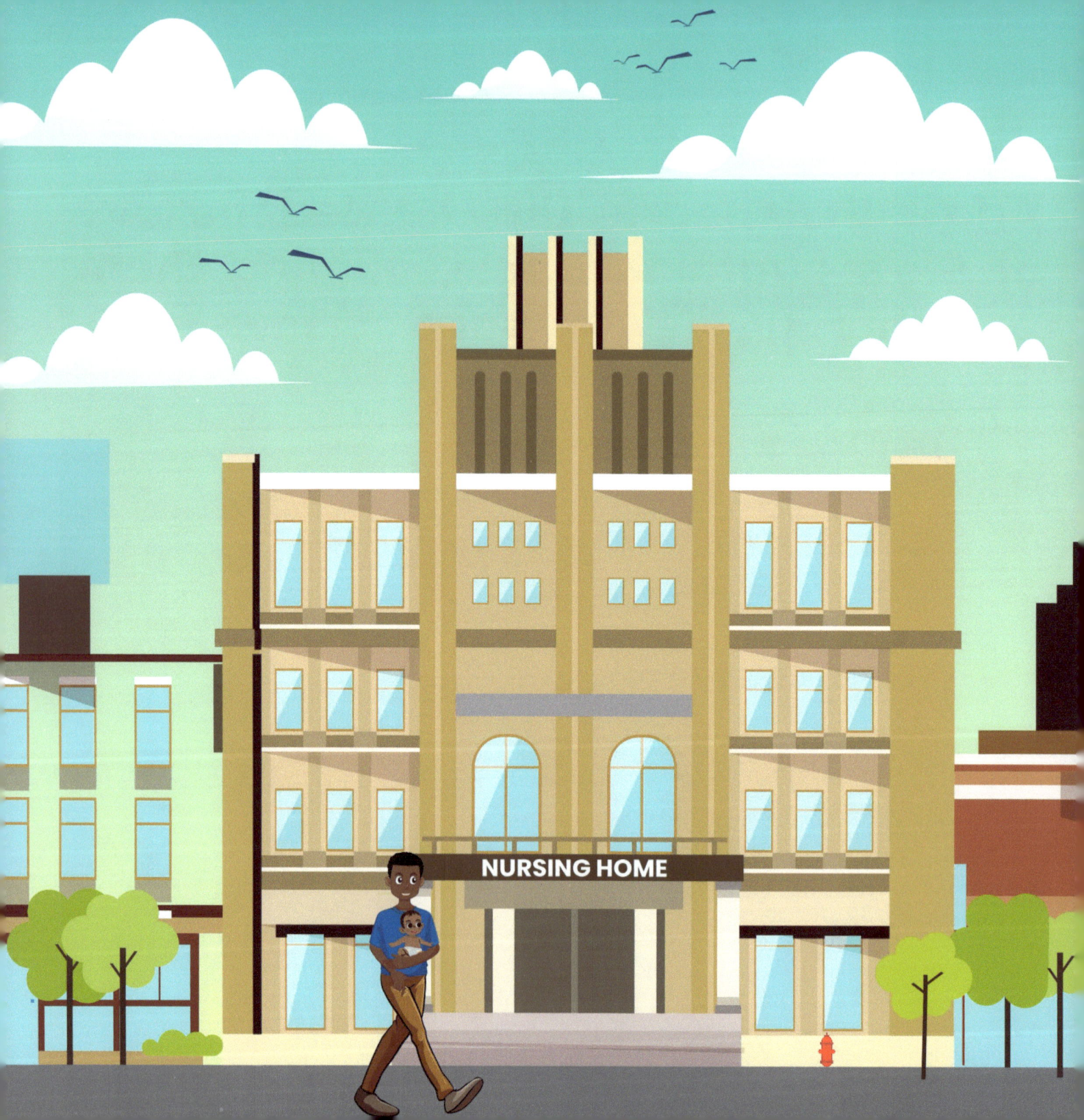

NURSING HOME

One day, Gio and his child decided to spread the love they had learned from the Bible.They visited a nursing home, bringing smiles and joy to the elderly residents.

They also helped their neighbors, lending a helping hand and showing kindness to those in need.

Together, they joined a community garden, planting seeds of hope and watching as their efforts blossomed into a beautiful garden of unity.

They spent time volunteering at a local shelter, serving meals and offering comfort to those who were less fortunate.

Inspired by their actions, the people of the town joined Gio and his child in organizing a charity event, raising funds to support a cause close to their hearts.

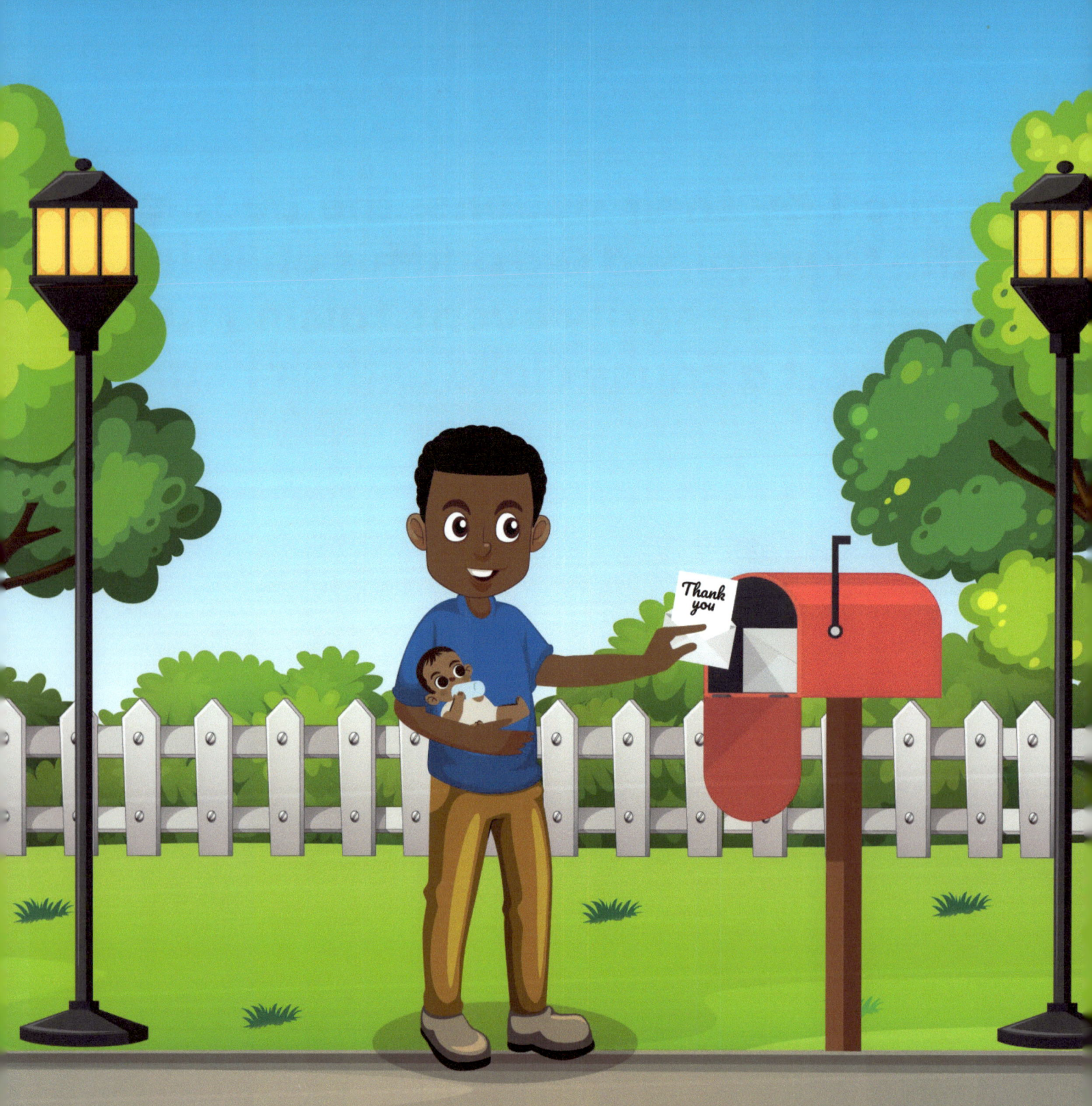

As they continued their acts of love and kindness, Gio and his child received heartfelt thank-you letters, reminding them of the impact they were making.

One day, Gio and his child sat under the tree where Gio and Ebony used to read the Bible. They shared stories and memories, feeling the presence of Gio's guardian angel.

As they looked up at the stars, Gio and his child felt a deep sense of connection to their loved ones, knowing that their love would always guide them.

The townspeople, inspired by Gio's journey, joined hands with Gio and his child, forming a circle of love and unity, spreading kindness and compassion throughout the town.

And so, the town continued to be filled with love and laughter, as Gio's guardian angel watched over them all.

Dear reader, may you always remember the power of love and the impact you can make in the lives of others. Spread kindness, just like Gio and his guardian angel, and watch as your actions create a world filled with love and light.

This book belongs to

_____

THE END

Educational Value:

"Gio's Guardian Angel" introduces young readers to the concept of faith and the teachings found in the Bible, fostering an understanding and appreciation for different belief systems.

The book emphasizes the values of love, kindness, and compassion, encouraging children to practice empathy and make a positive impact in their communities.

Through Gio's journey, readers learn about resilience and the ability to overcome challenges with the help of loved ones and inner strength. The story promotes the importance of intergenerational relationships, highlighting the wisdom and guidance that can be passed down from one generation to the next.

The book encourages readers to explore the wonders of nature, such as stargazing and appreciating the beauty of the world around them.

"Gio's Guardian Angel" instills a sense of hope and optimism, reminding readers that love is a powerful force that can bring joy and unity to individuals and communities.

www.ingramcontent.com/pod-product-compliance
Lightning Source LLC
Chambersburg PA
CBHW041554120626
46551CB00002B/207